LEADING THE
EMPATHIC
AGILE
ENTERPRISE

Leading the Empathic Agile Enterprise
Gail Ferreira

1. Title 2. Author 3. Agile, Leadership

Library of Congress Control Number: 2021901298
ISBN 13: 978-0-578-84596-8

LEADING THE
EMPATHIC
AGILE
ENTERPRISE

GAIL FERREIRA

Prima Leader, Inc.

Contents

Introduction

In hard times and not, running a business can be a difficult task. Oftentimes, when things start to fall apart, a leader may have no real idea of precisely where he failed. The leader may be a good manager, an excellent administrator, and a top-flight businessman, yet something seems to be missing in the equation.

This is where empathic leadership comes in.

So what *is* empathic leadership? Is it being sympathetic to the other person's point of view? Is it having an unseen intuition for what is going on around you? Or is it simply the refined skill of critical listening? The answer is that it is all of these. Leading with empathy is a bit of a loose term, but you will recognize empathic leadership once you see it. The purpose of this book is to give you a better feel for how to lead with empathy and to enumerate the advantages of doing so.

You as a leader need to listen with more than your ears. To get the most productivity out of your corporate family, you need to listen with your heart, your mind, and your gut as well. You need to be more aware of the unvoiced cues that your employees have been giving you as their souls cry out. Sometimes what your people are *not* telling you is at least as important as what they are.

That is the crux of empathic leadership.

Why Does Empathic Leadership Matter?

So why does my leadership style really matter anyway? How is the ability to be more empathetic toward one's employees going to make or break a company? The goal, after all, is to increase the bottom line, and that means doing whatever you can to attract and keep customers and lower your costs. Nothing else matters, right?

Don't get me wrong, satisfying the customers is very important, and lowering your costs for doing business is essential as well, but the effect that the mindset of your employees can have on your business goes far beyond what you put in their paychecks. They are people, not machines that can be fixed with a wrench and some grease, which makes the goal more complicated.

Visualize the working environment from the employees' point of view. Oftentimes, workers view their employers and upper management as simply kings and queens sitting up in their ivory towers, disconnected from the peasants below. Leaders often show little sensitivity for the condition of those they "rule" (as opposed to "lead'), what their subordinates feel, or anything about their employees' day-to-day duties. These ivory-tower rulers seem uncaring of the nuances of their workers' conditions and environment. An employee oftentimes feels that she could work herself into a grave and no one would care. With such little regard given them, why then would these employees give forth their best efforts to the company? Why should they do anything but the minimum expected of their job description?

For instance, suppose you have a leader trying to cut some costs here and there, and as part of that overall goal, the employee break room loses its microwave, or music that employees enjoy listening to on their breaks is no longer piped in. Loss of a way to heat food means some workers will now be bringing a cold sack lunch or will have to fork over extra dough and take time from their break to hoof it over to the local sandwich shop to pay money they didn't want to spend. And no music on their break? How are they supposed to relax? Lack of music can produce grumpy workers who display that grumpiness in the form of decreased productivity, and *that* affects the bottom line. In pinching a few pennies without being aware of employees' needs and desires, the unempathic leader will lose much more than she gains.

If the leader cares so little about her workers, then those workers will not care as much about what they're doing. Workers may then make mistakes that will cost time, money, and effort. People may even get hurt because other employees aren't caring enough about how they're doing their job, which means workers' comp at the least. Productivity will drop, which means higher costs and lower profit. Ultimately, all this can lead to a significant hit on a company's bottom line.

In the agile business community, of which I have been a part for the past fifteen to twenty years, the emphasis is on customer value, in finding ways of increasing that return on investment and measuring value in terms of dollars in versus dollars out. But this misses the larger picture. Customer value is important, yes, but so are other outside environmental factors, including the employees upon which the foundation of the company rests.

Without a proper foundation, even the strongest of organizations risks the possibility of collapse.

What Difference Does Empathic Leadership Make?

We've defined the problem, but how can being a more empathic leader solve that problem?

An empathic leader is more aware of *everything* around them, not just the numbers on the ledger. They are more sensitive to the human inputs crying out for attention, and are able to use their sixth sense, as it were, to develop that empathic muscle and become a better leader.

To use our previous example, suppose before making those cuts to streamline the budget, instead of a leader eating her own lunch up in the ivory tower's executive cafeteria, she takes a bit of time to walk around the worker areas. Then she might step into the break room and see how much use that microwave gets, or notice how relaxed her employees are with music playing and how it keeps them more cheerful and willing to put more effort into their jobs. When the employer takes notice of her employees' needs, she might think twice about cutting break room resources.

Employees want to be inspired, but that's not something an employer can do without stretching those empathic muscles and keeping an ear open to the work environment beneath her. Especially in a post-COVID environment, employees need a reason to show up for work all bright-eyed and bushy tailed. They need a reason not simply to get the work done but to feel like they are part of an extended family that requires their support and input.

Especially in a business where competition is fierce, how you lead your employees and those beneath you can be the make-or-break component of your management decisions.

Why Is Empathic Leadership Important in the Workplace?

Empathy goes beyond the leader and spreads like a plague throughout the employees. Setting an empathic environment begins with leaders demonstrating empathy to their employees, but once these employees notice their bosses demonstrating that they truly care about the guys in the trenches and are in the battle along with them, then some of that empathy begins to rub off. The employees then care more about the company as a whole, including the other workers, and respond by giving back to their employers.

A happy employee is more willing to assist the others around her when they need it and is more willing to roll up her sleeves and assist in areas where she normally wouldn't.

When an employer demonstrates that she cares for them, they in turn care more for others.

As an example, we could examine nearly any typical work environment where empathy is lacking: the cubicle-ridden office, for example. Everyone sticks to their own little cubicle, uncaring of the problems the coworker next to him is having. In fact, given a chance for a little backbiting and stepping on their neighbor to get ahead, most of the cubicle jockeys will grab it in a flash. How many such environments have you seen where someone is trying to portray a fellow worker in a bad light with HR simply so she can get the valued promotion instead? In an environment lacking empathy, a worker may prefer to allow the nearby coworker who has a problem to fail, and then leap in afterward as the perceived savior, never mind if that ends up costing the company a whole lot of extra money, as long as the employee gets what she wants for herself. Lack of empathy breeds an environment of selfishness.

Now introduce a more empathic leadership into that picture. If the main boss is more willing to listen to those underneath him, more willing to do what he can for their problems and treats everyone like a person instead of an entry in a ledger, then the workers in those cubicles will be happier and more willing to help coworkers who have a need. They will not automatically succumb to the level of backbiting as the way to get ahead. If everyone is rewarded for what they do and is working in a less stressful environment, they will feel less inclined to pass that stress along to someone else.

Back in 2017, 20% of U.S. employers offered empathy training for their managers, while in a more recent survey of 150 CEOs, over 80% saw empathy as a key ingredient to success. An increasing number of business leaders realize that empathy is not simply a vague touchy-feely hippie thing from the 60s, but a solid component to a productive and happy work environment.

Chapter One:

Traits of an Empathic Leader

What are the characteristics of an empathic leader, and how much of being empathic is art versus science? Well, truth be told, it's a little bit of both. Part sixth sense and part psychology, empathy is a skill you can train yourself to have. Some people are born with more empathy, true, but anyone with a willing attitude can improve their own empathic skill set. You simply have to be aware of what traits constitute an empathic leader and make an effort to emulate those traits.

It begins by saying to yourself, "I will try to be more empathetic."

Innate or Learned?

Emotional empathy has been found to be a genetic trait, one built in the early developmental years and molded by parents and other adults in a person's life. In this sense it is an inherent ability, an inborn sixth sense.

But even if you weren't born with the gift, you can still cultivate it within yourself by simply being more consciously aware of what traits constitute empathic leadership. Even for those born with the gift, not being aware of how it is manifested is a bit like having a car without the owner's manual . . . or driving the car without a driver's license.

Empathy is part art and part science. The science portion can be broken down into the components of what it means to be empathic in the role of being a leader. These components, these *traits*, can then be studied and learned so that no matter how lacking you may feel that you are in the way of inborn empathy, you can still cultivate it within yourself and make of yourself a more intuitive leader.

All you need to do is be aware of what traits constitute an empathic leader . . . which leads us to the next section.

Traits

So which traits constitute an empathic leader? There *is* a list, which is where we get into the science side of empathic leadership. The traits are not difficult, and are ones that any of us can work toward emulating. In no particular order, empathic leadership is comprised of the following traits:

➤ A Leader Is Self-Aware

An empathic leader knows themselves, their strengths and weaknesses, and how best to make use of each. Too many people don't even exemplify this first trait. How many people have you seen, for instance, that refuse to admit to their obvious weaknesses? They refuse to acknowledge any shortcomings, thinking the refusal makes them appear more strong, yet they succeed only in showcasing their weaknesses, usually at inopportune moments.

For instance, if you know that your strong suit is overseeing production but find yourself lacking in marketing, then focus on the former and hire a marketing specialist for the latter. It's better than trying to do it all yourself when you know you're not up to it. The alternative, after spending all that time and effort in getting the product up and running, is a marketing disaster because you insisted on doing everything yourself. Don't be a hero; play smart.

➤ A Leader Knows Self-Control

Panicking has caused many leaders to lose battles throughout history, while losing one's temper has started many wars. An empathic leader must exemplify self-control. No matter how bad a situation is, no matter how dire it may seem, an empathic leader knows how to keep her cool. Breathe, relax, and keep a level head, for that is the only way you will ever be able to see a way out of whatever crisis you're stuck in. Panicking and negative emotions tend to block logic, preventing the leader from calmly seeing what may be the only way out. In fact, a panicked person is ever only able to see what will *not* work.

Flying off the handle will only gain you a more negative environment and uncomfortable workers. If an employee made a big mistake, screaming at him for half an hour is not going to make him willing to do better; instead, his likely reaction will be to symbolically crawl in a corner and try not to be noticed. If anything, the other employees overhearing your tirade are going to feel equally uncomfortable and will be more likely to keep to themselves instead of being more helpful to others and the company as a whole. No one wants to be noticed if they know that the reward is going to be a screaming fit.

A better way to lead is to hold back that tirade, control yourself, and remain calm as you explain to the employee what she did wrong and why. If a crisis comes up, remain calm then as well. If your employees know you to be a calm, controlled, unflappable individual, they will be more willing to put their faith in you as a leader and remain loyal, productive workers.

On the other hand, no one ever had any faith in a weak, panic-stricken leader.

➢ Leaders Are More Hands-On

An empathic leader should be more hands-on, not only with the people above him but with those below him as well. A hands-on person is more willing to interact with employees throughout the organization and with other departments.

For instance, if there is a work stoppage and you know it's not coming from your department, venture forth to other departments in the company to determine where the fault might lie. Then, once you find it, offer to help out that other department in whatever way that you can. This will show everyone in the company that you are there for the good of the whole, for everyone large and small. You will become known as a team player, which is a good example to set.

You must be more interactive. If all you're doing is sitting behind that desk signing papers all day, then you're never going to know what fires need to be put out; you will never be there to see the problems, much less be available to fix them. Stay informed about every aspect of the company's proceedings as well as its employees; then you'll be in a better position to spot that crisis forming before it happens and nip it in the bud.

➢ Exterior Perspectives

An empathic leader is also confident enough to seek other perspectives. Knowing what's going on in other departments, with the employees, is a good start, but *why* do they do what they do? What is the reason that others have the systems they do? Keep an ear to the ground.

For instance, you may hear that one department is imploding due to the tyrannical, mean-spirited actions of its manager, but is reporting him to get him replaced always the answer? If in the past he was a good, solid manager, be curious to find out what changed. Maybe he's going through a divorce, or maybe a favorite aunt died. Whatever the reason behind the personal crisis, the manager's failed efforts to keep the problem in and deal with it behind the scenes is bringing his entire department down. Get an eye into his perspective, the reason behind his actions, and maybe you can help him through it and as a side effect bring the whole department back up to full productivity.

Or suppose you're new to an organization and have noticed some odd way a department completes a particular task. You would want to find out right away the why behind their method instead of simply accepting and copying the actions of others. Is there a good reason behind their actions that you can learn from? Or maybe the reason for doing things that way was once a good one, but now you happen to know of a different, better way that would streamline the organization as a whole. Either way, it's important to examine these exterior perspectives.

And then, of course, attempt to learn what others think about *you*. Are you really doing the great job you thought you were, or does it turn out that the employees view *you* as the office tyrant? Perspective is everything.

➤ A Leader Is Creative

A leader is creative, with that out-of-the-box mentality that has defined many a great entrepreneur. She is able to see beyond the usual solutions to a path that leads to greater than expected success. She is creative enough to see solutions to problems that people are not even aware exist.

Take, for example, Steve Jobs. Oftentimes he would develop a product that no one even knew they would need. The whole point-and-click GUI environment of modern computers was something being developed by Xerox but sidelined as a wasteful endeavor; the same idea was ignored by IBM as a passing fad for several years until well after the Apple computer hit the market.

Or the cell phone? How many people foresaw the need to have a phone in their pocket? Then later when phones evolved into the pocket computer that is the iPhone, who could have foreseen that anyone would care to browse the web or send text messages while away from home?

Society never previously saw a need for these capabilities, but a creative mind realized the need before it was apparent. The results, as they say, are legend and catapulted Apple into the stratosphere.

Creativity can also engender creative solutions to organizational processes. Back to the example of a department that's having trouble with a tyrannical manager, the solution may be that the division needs to be separated into *two* departments, one of which has a label the company has never used before. Or perhaps there's a better way of running the factory production line that flies in the face of traditional methods but nevertheless gets the job done far more efficiently. In fact, the whole idea of an "assembly line" was one such radical creative idea thought up by old Henry Ford.

Being creative, being innovative, and keeping an ear to that sixth sense will both inspire employees as well as build productivity.

Identifying an Empathic Leader

How, then, can you identify empathic leadership in others? Simply be on the lookout for the following traits:

- Self-Aware
- Self-Control
- Hands-on
- Exterior Perspectives
- Creativity

Of course, if you need a good mnemonic for remembering these traits, I have a simple one:

- Self-**C**ontrol
- **H**ands-on
- Self-**A**ware
- **C**reativity
- **E**xterior Perspectives.

"CHACE." It may be spelled incorrectly, but the acronym is easy to remember.

Remember, though, that we're talking empathic "leaders." Be aware of what's going on with others around you, both with your employees and the company, but do not make the mistake of getting bogged down by all the discord. You must train yourself to be aware of the problems and states of mind of others while not internalizing them or you risk the possibility of burning yourself out. And a burnt-out executive can lead no one at all.

A good leader must find his balance, and that is what differentiates an empath from an empathic leader; an empathic leader knows where the line must be drawn and knows how to listen without going deaf. You must still be able to lead, but be aware of what and who it is that you lead; keep your fingers in the pie without becoming the pie.

Chapter Two:

Advantages

Now that we have identified what it means to be an empathic leader, we will discuss the advantages of empathic leadership in the workplace. How can empathy, or the lack thereof, make or break even the biggest of corporations? How can empathy drive a small company operating out of someone's garage into something far greater?

Let's examine the concept in a bit more detail.

Advantages of Empathic Leadership

There are several real-world advantages to be had from empathic leadership. And the advantages are important enough to carry an organization through both lean times and good, enabling the company to weather the economic storms that everyone must face. A list of advantages includes:

19

➤ Empathic Leaders Are Adaptable

A leader who is in tune with her employees, the company, and the business environment in general is one who is adaptable to changing circumstances. Especially in a market where competition is high and the environment can change overnight, navigating the business world can be a bit like shooting the rapids and equally dangerous. Failing to act quickly enough could put you at the bottom of the market. But an empathic leader in tune with her environment can more readily adapt to changing times.

The reason an empathic leader is more adaptable is because such a leader is in tune with her people and will know how far she can trust them, whether they will have her back, and who would be best for a given new assignment. She will be able to make key decisions much more quickly since she will already be in the know of the nitty-gritty details of her people, as well as of the market in general.

For example, suppose the market is toys, specifically bobbleheads. Currently bobbleheads for one set of characters are quite popular, but then the next great thing comes out and suddenly the market for those particular bobbleheads bottoms out. Now you have a warehouse full of bobbleheads that no one's going to buy. How does being an adaptable empathic leader apply to this scenario?

The empathic leader realizes the fact that the market for those bobbleheads will last only as long as the initial popularity for that movie will, so he keeps an eye open for the next movie coming down the pike; he watches how the interests of people in the street wax and wane and readies production to be ready to ramp up for the next generation of bobbleheads on a moment's notice. Then when that new movie comes out and popularity changes, he already has a solution ready and is able to hit the market while other companies are still trying to sell the old bobbleheads that now no one wants.

The empathic leader is constantly adapting, constantly in flux and agile. He's ready for anything.

➤ Happier Workers

Employees that feel valued and appreciated are more likely to pass along that same attitude to others they work with, who in turn will feel safer and happier with their coworkers and will continue to pass the attitude of general good feelings along to others in their environment. Before you know it, the empathic leader has created a culture of happy, productive workers in her company.

Happy workers are also far less likely to call in sick when they aren't, and are far more committed to the task at hand. Their morale is higher, they go about their duties with a bounce in their step, and have far more energy in everything they do. These qualities translate into greater productivity.

Happy workers show more team spirit, fewer workplace disruptions, and less reason to complain to HR or their lawyer.

➤ Empathic Leaders Engender Employee Loyalty

If employees know that their boss is trustworthy, caring, and relatable, if they know that here is a person who will have their backs and respects them, then they are far more likely to remain loyal to that person and hence the company in general.

This outcome is not only good for worker output but counters the brain drain that can occur between companies. When a slightly better offer comes to an employee from a competing company, he will consider how much loyalty he feels for the ones who have had his back and will think twice before leaving a company where he feels so comfortable.

Staff loyalty means that you get to keep the good talent that built your company in the first place, and that is *always* a good outcome.

➢ Empathic Leaders Spur General Creativity

Just as one of the traits of an empathic leader is to be creative, setting an example of out-of-the-box thinking can encourage others to be equally creative, to be unafraid of intuiting solutions and innovations that buck the standard model, solutions that may have been frowned upon in other, more restrictive environments.

Because employees working under an empathic leader feel more a part of the organization, like a family member instead of a drone, they are more inclined to equate the company's success with their own. This means they will be ready and willing to help innovate, to follow the example in creativity that their manager showed them by way of his own actions. Employees who feel leadership lends a listening ear to their ideas will feel a sense of self-satisfaction that engenders loyalty.

For instance, back to our bobblehead example, if the empathic manager has been saying that she expects the market to turn and to be on the lookout for the next big bobblehead character, one employee could offer up something like, "Hey, there's this one book that my kid and his friends absolutely adore and there's supposed to be a movie based on it coming out in a couple of months. Sounds like it'd be really popular." A manager who is willing to listen to their employees' ideas has the advantage of an inside scoop to be ready when the market turns. In a more restrictive environment, a low-level employee is unlikely to volunteer their idea, especially if they know they will never receive any credit for the suggestion or even be ridiculed.

➤ Increased Communication

Some companies are so big, sprawling, and inflexible that no one in one department knows what any of the other departments are doing. Communication falters, and in particularly toxic environments, no one shares with anyone across departments. With an empathic leader spreading empathy throughout the corporation, however, communication is more open and free, people are far more likely to speak up about a problem or possible solution they might have, and the whole system flows much more smoothly. Communication bottlenecks that bring production to a grinding halt are a relic of the past.

How important is communication? In any sort of organization, it is one of the key ingredients of a successful day-to-day operation. Better internal communication means a corporate ability to more swiftly deal with any issue that arises.

➤ People Feel Safer

Safety is particularly important in these COVID-19 panic-stricken times. Workers in an organization run by an empathic leader trust their leader, and by extension, as we have seen, the organization as a whole and all within it. They trust that the company will see after their benefit in good times and in bad, allowing them to remain focused on the work at hand.

Then, when something like a pandemic comes around, they know the company cares about their safety and that leadership will make sure that the workplace remains a secure environment for its employees. The workers know that the company will continue to provide them with what is required to keep them going safely and efficiently.

Disadvantages of Lack of Empathy

Let us now examine what happens in a corporation that lacks empathy. What disadvantages might a company incur, and how severe will be those handicaps?

➤ Rigidity

Any organization lacking an empathic culture is going to instead have a resistant one. Managers will be afraid to be the first to suggest a change operations, employees will have no incentive to volunteer any of their own suggestions, and the corporate structure will be unable to adapt to critically changing times. Such cultures tend to be inflexible and as such have a tendency to die an early death.

Take the bobblehead example once again. In reference to an employee who offers an idea for a future popular bobblehead, the inflexible manager might think, "I'm not going to bet this company's future on what some guy's kid thinks might be popular in a few months." The end result of that attitude would then be a warehouse full of old bobbleheads that no one wants and a big red mark on the company ledger.

➤ It's Only a Paycheck

If workers don't care about their job, as will often happen in a corporation that lacks empathic leadership, then it becomes just a way to earn another paycheck. Employees do only what is expected of them and nothing else, with a complete lack of enthusiasm. People rarely participate in any company functions and have low morale, because after all, they are only there to earn another paycheck, nothing else.

In fact, oftentimes you will see employees knocking off from work early to partake in something of greater importance than that "dumb job." Ever see a workplace where three guys are standing around chatting with the one guy going at a sluggish work pace? That's a sure sign of workers who don't care about their job beyond earning a paycheck. Their hearts simply aren't in their jobs.

➢ No Company Loyalty

Company loyalty can be important. Without it, talented people will look for any reason to leave for a better-paying job at a competing company, thus siphoning off what talent a company has. That sort of brain drain has killed off many a good company to foreign competition.

➢ Generally Toxic Environment

Unhappy, distrustful workers afraid to speak up except through the mouth of a lawyer if they feel the company has slighted them, managers who care little for their employees and the employees know it, a workplace where no one talks to or cares about anyone else—all this can make for a very toxic environment and distressed employees. Such stresses can lead to medical bills happily billed to the company the people work for, fighting between cubicles, and workers calling in sick simply to get away from it all.

No one can work in that sort of toxic environment, so productivity will plummet, and ultimately valuable, talented employees will leave for a better organization the first chance they get.

➢ No One Feels Safe

In an age where people are in a panic over a pandemic, how likely do you think that the workers will be excited to return to the office when the company tells them it's safe to return to work after a proven track record of not having their employees' backs during good times? Short of being promised a hazmat suit, workers are more likely to stay home and unproductive until well after the crisis has passed.

➢ Stagnation

While empathic leadership can encourage creativity, a lack of such leadership can result in creative stagnation. The line, "If it was good for my grandfather's time, it's good enough for me," becomes the company motto. Nothing changes, and you're metaphorically still trying to market those bobbleheads from a movie that was popular years ago.

Now that we understand the advantages and disadvantages of leading empathically, we shall next discuss *how* to lead empathically.

Chapter Three:

How to Lead Empathically

Being an effective empathic leader requires one key skill: listening. It also requires one key realization: workers are people too.

Whether employer or employee, don't forget that both are human, all with the same needs and considerations. It's a variation of the old Golden Rule: Do unto others as you would have them do unto you. Imagining yourself in their place, how would you feel about what you're doing to them? Would such an action make you more or less productive? Would you want to quit? Well, why should they feel any less than you would if the situation were reversed?

Let's examine what it means to be an empathic leader.

Empathic Leadership Is a Responsibility

Being a leader is a responsibility, not a free ride. In the military, the motto is "Officers eat last" because officers prefer to operate with a servant-based leadership system, thereby acknowledging that their men are at least as important as they are. Because when you're in the trenches getting shot at, you have to absolutely trust the guy next to you; it literally means your life.

Compare that to how close a relationship the typical manager has with those underneath him. Are you ever in the trenches with your employees? If a situation comes up, do you assign someone to go handle it, then go off to relax in the executive lounge? Or do you hold all calls and get your hands dirty by working alongside your employees until the crisis has been handled?

In short, if you're not in the trenches with your employees, then they won't be there for you. A good leader is the first one in the office in the morning and the last one to leave at night.

Active Listening

The primary skill of an empathic leader is *listening.* Learn to listen with your ears, with your gut, and with your heart, because people don't always say what is wrong with them; sometimes you have to see or feel what's bothering them. Has their mood suddenly changed? Is someone looking more downcast than before? Or when you walk into the employees' lounge, how does the mood feel?

This brings up an important aspect to active listening: do you *ever* check out the employees' lounge? It is impossible to listen to your employees if you don't expose yourself to their concerns. Walk with them, talk with them, or sometimes take a brief stroll through the hall of cubicles to get a feel for the mood. To *listen* to your employees, you need to *be* with your employees, sharing some of the same workplace experiences that may be causing them pain.

I have mentioned how important it is to listen with more than your ears. People can be screaming their dissatisfaction by the way they operate and look yet not say a word about it. That fake smile plastered across their face may be hiding a world of pain. These are the cues that you need to listen to, because believe it or not, the truly dissatisfied never submit anything to the suggestions box. They just suddenly quit one day.

Listen then to what is *not* said, more than what is said.

Ask the Key Questions

A key part of active listening is knowing what questions to ask some of your people to trigger an insightful reply.

Powerful questions will provide helpful answers. And beyond the words spoken, listen to employees' voice tone and note any tell-tale gestures.

A simple example of a powerful question would be, "What matters most?" I have used this many times in my coaching sessions. The answer might be a simple, "Well, my job, of course," or "The good of the company," but those are simply standard answers the employee expects that you want to hear. That is why you need to follow up with variations on a theme, then compare each answer and the way in which it is spoken to help you get to the core of what drives this person and how you can get an answer that can help them help themselves. Follow-ups like, "No, what *really* matters to you? Personally?"

Knowing how and when to ask a question can be as illuminating as listening to the answer itself.

Workers Are Human

Never forget that your employees are not just entries on a ledger, not simply cogs in a machine. They are human, and they need to be reminded of that from time to time. Take away their humanity and you take away their reason for caring for the well-being of your company and for why they should work hard. Or work at all.

The little things matter. For instance, do you allow little homey touches in the break room? Do you have a system whereby you let the employees choose (within reason) the music? Do you greet them by name when you pass them by in the hall, or do you even bother to get to *know* their names? Do you offer simple courtesies such as saying "thank you" or "well done" when they deserve recognition? Try this: The first time in the morning when you pass someone, ask how they're doing, and *listen* and *react* to the answer instead of simply giving lip-service to it. "Hey Fred, how'd your kid's ball game turn out?" or "Congratulations on that award."

When times are lean, are you the first to suggest firing people as a means of cutting back? Or do you remember that your employees are more than simply resources, that they have families and perhaps there may be other ways to tighten the belt?

You're a Human Too

Oftentimes people need to know that the ones above them are human as well—that they make the same sorts of mistakes, share the same kinds of pain. Never try to put yourself up there like some infallible monarch, because then when comes the fall, it'll be a hard one and there'll be no one left around to help you out or even feel sorry for you.

If you're the one who made a mistake that cost the company something, then admit it instead of trying to find a scapegoat. Just go out there and give a quick little speech. Something like, "Hey, people, I know it's been rough and we've all been working hard, but this last one's on me. I filed the wrong form with the government and as a result we suffered. Responsibility's all mine." That will let them know that you're just as human as they are and that you take your own errors as seriously as theirs.

Contrary to popular belief, not even the best of us are infallible. Workers, managers, doctors, and presidents—all have an equal chance of making a mistake, of being fallible. That includes you. What's more, the ones working under you are well aware of this, and any attempt you try to make it seem like a problem is not your fault simply undermines your authority in their eyes. They know you're only human, so act like it.

Be There for Your People

There's a reason why you're in upper management, and that's because of your greater experience and skill sets. If not, then you would be working *under* some of your employees instead of *over* them. Knowing this, a good leader should be quite willing to share some of that experience to those employees who need it.

If you see an employee having a problem with something that used to give *you* chills back in the day, something you have since learned the trick to get around, then take a minute or two to tell that employee the better way of doing it. Don't wait for them to come to you, because they'll be too embarrassed to admit to their failings. Keep the tone even and not accusatory; remember that people listen more to those who speak *with* them, not *at* them. If you have the time, you might even keep the conversation casual. Say something like, "Boy, I remember when that used to give me migraines. Have you tried it this way?"

Just remember that it wasn't all that long ago when you were in their place.

As a leader, your job is to guide, to help everyone move forward because one person held back means the whole job is held back. That means being there for each and every one of your people, not just yelling at them to "shape up or ship out."

Provide Feedback

People need some sort of sign that you've actually heard what they were trying to tell you, a follow-up that indicates their boss truly heard and understands their problems, some actionable content. This reaction will tell them more, surely than anything else, that they really are part of a family that cares for its own.

For example, that microwave in the break room. It's on its last legs; everyone has told you so. Would it really put the company out all that much to spring for a new one? Then the next day the employees walk in for their first break, and lo and behold they see this shiny new microwave oven. No big fanfare, you just *do*.

Or back to the bobbleheads. The idea the one employee suggested to have the next set of bobbleheads based on a forthcoming kids movie turns out to be an astounding success. Rather than taking credit for it all yourself, post a simple notice along the lines of, "Charles Alexander had a great idea with those bobbleheads. Excellent job, Charlie! Your bonus is in the mail."

Whatever form of feedback you give to show that you've been listening to what your people have to say, remember that actions speak louder than words.

Create a Circle of Safety

Your employees need to feel safe at their place of employment—free of any danger not only from outside the company but especially from within it. They need not fear the threat of pitting one employee against another. They must feel that they're all part of the same team, all in it together. They must feel valued by their colleagues and employers alike. They must feel about them a circle of safety.

Then, when hard times come, they will at least feel safe when it comes to their jobs and not be stressed out from that source. They will continue to work their best because they know that they will be safe. After all, all employees want the same thing: a place where they feel physically and psychologically safe.

To establish this circle of safety, you need only follow the other points mentioned in this chapter. Make sure employees understand that it is perfectly okay to approach you with candid feedback; after all, there was a time in the distant past when you were the one daring to give your boss suggestions, both good and bad. Engage in active listening with all your senses to hear what your employees have to say. Then remember to offer feedback, and always thank the person for opening up to you. Never angrily rebuke what they suggested, but rather make sure that you understand their perspective and ask any questions you need to make sure you're clear about things.

Once this circle of safety is firmly established, then your people will be *your people* and pull together as a team through thick and thin.

Don't Be Afraid of Uncertainty

A leader must not be afraid of the uncertain. Rather, she must be ready to face it, and she does this by being prepared, in the sense of knowing what and who she has to work with. She is prepared by having engendered that circle of safety and knowing that whatever she faces, her employees will be there to face it with her.

When faced with uncertainty, an empathic leader will be ready to deal with an issue, whether it be something the company as a whole faces or simply something more localized that a small group of employees is having to deal with.

Consider uncertainty a new challenge to be met. When your employees see you facing this challenge, that will inspire the confidence that you'll both need to carry on.

I've Got Your Back; You've Got Mine

What all this adds up to is a simple statement that you are, in essence, making to your employees in actions more than words: "I've got your back."

There is no more fundamental a way of expressing your support; it all comes down to the way you tell them. And your way should be *showing* more than telling.

Once your employees get your message and believe it to be true, then they'll send back their own response, again in actions more than words: "And we've got yours."

Once you can make it through those two simple sentences, then you are leading empathically, and both those working under you and your bottom line will thank you.

Leading empathically is not simply a matter of stating, "People, from now on I am going to be more empathetic." Rather, it is a matter of showing by action, to which your employees will respond in kind.

Chapter Four:

LEAD–Formula for Leadership

Leading by empathy is best summed up by the word itself: Lead. More specifically, an acronym that sums up everything you need to remember. LEAD stands for:

Lead side by side

Empathy Mapping

Adapt (Cynefin)

Discipline

Let's review each of these one by one.

Lead Side by Side

The best leaders throughout history were ones that were there in the dirt with their people. These are the ones who realized that they couldn't simply sit back and let others do everything themselves. They were needed to supervise, yes, to keep abreast of the whole picture, but they always remembered that they were **part** of the team. A leader works *with* his people, not *over* them.

The difference here is key. If a problem arises, you are right there with the rest, ready to handle it on the spot; no delays on word getting to you, no time spent going through channels or employees having to work up the nerve to tell the big guy that something's gone wrong.

Back to the bobblehead example again. Something happens on the production line that brings work to a halt. Now, if you've stuck yourself up in your ivory tower all day and left someone else to handle "all the little problems," it might be after lunch break before you find out about the problem, and your command on how to fix it might even be further delayed before that information filters down to the factory floor. On the other hand, if you're a manager who takes regular walk-throughs of the factory level to make sure everything is going fine, you are more likely to be present at the moment the error occurs and can see it for yourself, which will help you to know immediately what must be done to get things working again.

Leading alongside your team is simply more efficient and engenders more a sense of teamwork in your people.

Empathy Mapping

An empathy map is a visual representation of how a person feels and thinks, a way of getting to the core of what someone is trying to tell you outside of their spoken words. In the past it has been used to view a customer's perspective on how they feel about a given product, but here I am using it to get a good look at a company's different employee personas. This allows me to see who is being handled properly, who is being sidelined or left out, and where the focus needs to turn for the organization to handle everyone equally. This tool allows me to determine what interventions may be necessary to make sure that *everyone* is as productive as they can possibly be.

An empathy map has four quadrants, each corresponding to a key trait. Each quadrant is then partitioned off into various squares that correspond to a type of persona within that organization. The four quadrants are as follows:

- Say and do
- Think and feel
- See
- Hear

From there I color-code my empathy maps to have a different color represent each of the various types of personas listed on the map; this simply makes it easier to pick out what's what. These quadrants are in the behavioral section of the map.

Then alongside that there is the why section. This contains two quadrants:

- Wins/Gains
- Losses/Pains

These two quadrants tell us what the various persona types are thinking in the way of overall wins and losses.

Within each of the colored persona boxes are then listed some representative answers to key questions that I've asked of the employees during my interviews. No need to shuffle through piles of feedback forms; all the information is summed up on this one graphic. This makes for an easy-to-see summary of how successful your leadership really is.

How it works is the interviewer not only writes down an employee's answers but *how* the employee answers, what nonverbal cues they give that may be conveying more than the words spoken. What else did I observe about the employee and the environment around him? This is best summed up by this graphic:

Empathy Map

That is, of course, a very general outline of the process the interviewer goes through during the interview process to collect the data necessary to generate the empathy map. For the final result, here is a typical empathy map template that I use so you can see what I'm talking about:

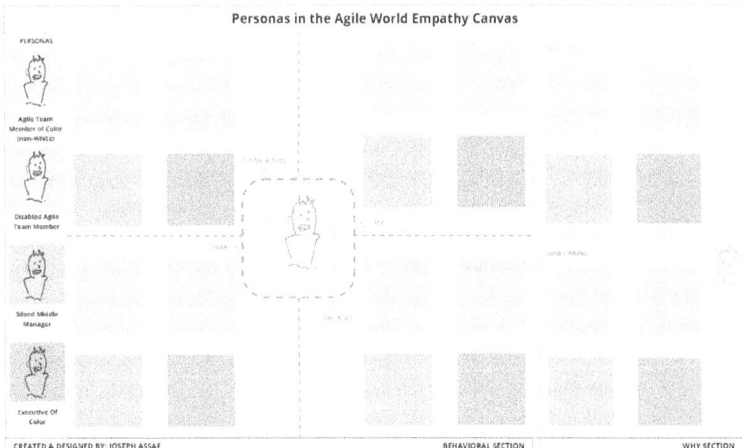

This is what I have used in many agile transformation strategy mapping sessions. To give you an idea of what it looks like filled out, I've also included an actual empathy map that I completed for a financial client when I worked with them to map out these personas for their employees using this template.

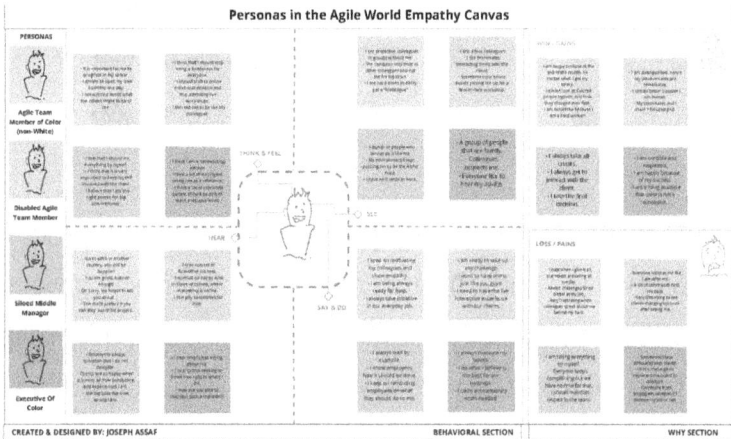

Empathy mapping can be a powerful tool to get a quick yet detailed look into your overall employee satisfaction and efficiency, as broken down by generalized persona categories and their own experiences.

Adapt (Cynefin)

Welsh for "habitat," Cynefin is a decision-making model that a manager can use to help him decide how to respond in a chaotic environment. The tool is essentially a visual guide to help a leader learn how to adapt. Since adaptability is one of the traits of an empathic leader, Cynefin helps with that adaptability by showing a leader what area they need to focus on. In a chaotic environment, you need to find the road that will take you to an area of stability and a final solution. This is what Cynefin helps you do.

The Cynefin framework is divided into 5 basic domains:

- Simple
- Complicated
- Complex
- Chaotic
- Disorder

Simple includes things that are obvious, that which is known—the "known knowns." These are easy to deal with because we know everything about them.

Complicated includes the "known unknowns"—those things where we know our knowledge fails but at least we know how to aim our efforts. For that which lies in this domain we need to gather more data, analyze it, then respond.

Complex represents the "unknown knowns." We have no idea what about a situation that we lack the knowledge of, so the only course is to keep probing and see what might work.

Chaotic represents that domain where cause and effect are unclear and issues are too confusing. The only way through this is to take an action—*any* action—and see what happens.

Disorder is what we are completely unclear about and can't even tell which domain applies. It may be a case of many domains overlapping or where factional leaders are arguing and no clear pattern is present. The only way out is to break a situation down into its constituent components to assign to each of the other domains, then to react appropriately on those components.

The following graphic illustrates what I mean:

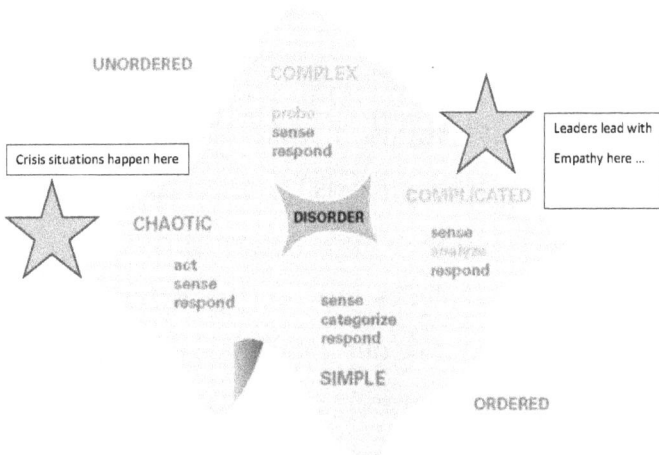

Once you have your problem broken down into these different domains, then you will have a far better idea of how to react to each segment in turn. Break it down, study what you need to do, and tackle one issue at a time instead of all at once. It's a template to show you how to adapt, as well as when you should do so and to what degree.

For example, suppose the problem with the bobblehead production line comes down to a feeder getting jammed. If this is something that has happened time and again, then you know how to handle it. You turn off the machine, send in Fred to pull out the wad of material that jammed up the works, then restart again. Total elapsed time is about ten minutes. This is a "simple" problem. If, however, there seems to be more to it than that and you don't know what's wrong, then you may have a "complex" problem. *That's* when you call up the repairman listed for the device and have them send out a guy for whom it *would* be a simple problem.

Break each problem down like that and you'll have less of a tendency to overreact or panic. You will know to what degree you will have to adapt.

Discipline

Once you have gone through all the inputs, examined what needs to be done, determined what given approaches work best for your organization, and know what to do, then you must have the wherewithal to stick with the plan. Even the best of programs does no good whatsoever if you don't follow it. This is where discipline comes in.

Break it down like this:

1. Observe: You're in data-taking mode here, checking out what's happening, what's going wrong, what's working and not.

2. Analyze: Once you have your raw data, it's time to analyze it. Find the reasons *why* things are going wrong, what specifics need to be attended to. Is it personnel? Management? Equipment? The company organizational structure? Pare it down to its base elements.

3. Decide: You know what needs to be fixed and why; now it's time to decide on what that fix entails. What new framework do you need to adapt? There are a ton of different frameworks and strategies out there to choose from; what you need to do is find the one that works for *your* organization. What strategy serves it best?

4. Stick to the plan: You have your new framework, your new company strategies and goals; now stick with

the plan. Have the discipline of a real leader to keep doing what you know works for your given situation.

Of course, if you've been staying very disciplined about keeping to your battle plan and something is still not working, that's where we hark back to being adaptable, returning to the first step of analyzing what else needs to be tweaked in our company structure.

That is the basic essence of LEAD. To be a good empathic leader, remember to lead by LEAD.

Chapter Five:

Real-Life Examples

People hear the word "empathic" and they equate that more with "touchy-feely" than "business success." But there are plenty of examples in the world that show it *is* possible to treat your employees like people and still have great success for your organization.

Need a few examples? How about any given episode of *Undercover Boss*?

The format of that show is the same for all. The CEO of a chain store is invited to spend some time out of his ivory tower to be in the trenches along with her employees. The boss is in disguise and thus has a chance to see what life is really like for her employees. Oftentimes the boss is shocked and moved by what she sees, and by the end of the segment when she reveals who she really is, she starts making changes based on what she experienced for herself.

The types of companies vary widely, but some of these are pretty large corporations. For example, there was an episode where the president and CEO of 7-Eleven went undercover and had a chance to see how hard his people work, the hardships they face personally and in the workplace, and how even a few simple changes on his part would make things a lot better for them. This is a perfect example of getting out into the trenches with your people and being more empathetic to their situations.

Leaders and CEOs from corporations ranging from White Castle, Hooters, and Waste Management to True Value, the city of Pittsburgh, and Cinnabon also took the leap into their employees' shoes. There was even one episode from the British version of the show where the mayor of a city had a chance to see what it was like as a city employee working by the rules his own office had set up.

These are not small companies but fairly large ones that are understandably concerned with the bottom line. In each case they cozy up alongside their employees on the sly and get to see for themselves what it's like in the trenches. Based on these experiences, many of those CEOs ended up making favorable changes for the welfare of their employees. Did that put them out of business? Certainly not. They are all still thriving to this day, some better than ever.

But above and beyond any others that I could list is one particular example I would name. This man is not only extremely successful but is generally well-liked by everyone in the business. He is everyone's favorite billionaire, Richard Branson.

Branson is quoted as saying that while he values his customers and has made customer service a top priority, he sees his employees as even more important. To quote:

"It should go without saying, if the person who works at your company is 100 percent proud of the brand and you give them the tools to do a good job and they are treated well, they're going to be happy." And in the end, he says, happy workers means happy customers.

When on flights of his own airline, he has gone so far as to walk the cabin and collect feedback, talking directly to the staff onboard the plane. You can't get much more "in the trenches" than that.

Among the specific points that Branson adheres to is to set the example of creativity; his own spirit of creative innovation inspires his employees to do the same. He has also said time and again that he takes care of his staff, because if your people are proud of their brand and are treated well, then they are going to pass that smiling face onto the customer. He's also not afraid to let people discover their own abilities, to give them the space to grow and thrive. He himself is not above admitting to his employees that he has made many mistakes himself, but to him they are learning experiences.

All of what he says and does comes from a place of empathic leadership, and you can't argue with the results. If one of the most successful people on the planet can buck the conventional wisdom and lead empathically and still be *that* successful, then anyone can do it.

Chapter Six:

Wrap-Up

Empathic leadership is all about listening with more than just your ears, of being aware of those unspoken messages your employees are trying to tell you. It means not forgetting that those who work *under* you are actually working *with* you. By remembering this simple reality, you can get far more out of your employees and make both them *and* your bottom line happy. There is no need to sacrifice your humanity to reach your corporate goals.

Empathy is both an art and a science, something some people are born with but that which we all can learn if we simply remain aware of the traits of an empathic leader by remembering the acronym CHACE:

- Self-**C**ontrol
- **H**ands-on
- Self-**A**ware

- Creativity
- Exterior Perspectives.

The advantages to empathic leadership include an adaptable organization, happier workers, loyal employees, greater creativity, increased communication, safer-feeling employees, and an ability to navigate even the roughest of management waters. Just remember to lead with LEAD, display confidence in your employees, and remember that you are *all* a part of the same team.

You are a leader, not a monarch.

www.ingramcontent.com/pod-product-compliance
Lightning Source LLC
Chambersburg PA
CBHW071022040426
42443CB00007B/905